Anxiety Recovery

The Guide to Overcoming Anxiety and Living Normally Again

ANDY KLOSS

ISBN: 9798784192011

Copyright Page

Anxiety Recovery: The Guide to Overcoming Anxiety and Living Normally
Again
© Andy Kloss 2021

For more information, email andy@andykloss.com.

CONTENTS

GET YOUR FREE GIFT

To get the best experience with this book, I highly recommend downloading and using my FREE Guided Meditation For Anxiety Relief which will help you reduce feeling overwhelmed, calm you down, and create a sense of ease.

You can download it by visiting:
andykloss.com/book-gift

FOREWORD

I am eternally grateful for the vicissitudes of life, for they brought me to where I am today.

Through the pain, I was forced to re-examine my life which put me on the path of personal growth and spirituality. It helped me find a deeper connection to our true nature beyond the physical form of our bodies and minds, also known as awareness or consciousness. My life has now taken on a beautiful and meaningful quality.

"If I have seen further than others, it is by standing upon the shoulders of giants."
Isaac Newton

My heart goes out to all the giants that allowed me to stand on their shoulders.

There have been so many giants in my life that it would be impossible to list them all here.

Some of them are mentioned throughout the book.

I would like to thank my mother for showing me what unconditional love means and my dad, who has always been there for me.

And to you, dear reader, thanks for reading this book, and may it serve you well in recovering from anxiety.

INTRODUCTION

According to "Our World In Data," 284 million people experienced an anxiety disorder globally in 2017.

It is my mission to help you overcome anxiety.

This book shares my personal philosophy, approach, and experience, having recovered naturally in three years. It took me a while to figure out how to recover, so it doesn't necessarily have to take you three years. Some people have had an anxiety disorder for decades and believe it is not possible to recover. If that is your case, I challenge you to consider whether that is a belief rather than the underlying reality.

It doesn't matter how long we have been suffering or what our story is; my personal experience has shown me that it is possible to recover. The problem we face is that we have not been taught how to handle emotional challenges, nor about the nature of emotion and thought.

This book is spiritual in nature, as all healing and recovery are spiritual. This work is not based on any religion but is compatible with all religions. It contains the essence of that to which all religions point.

It's funny; I used to not be spiritual at all. Self-help was also something that was not part of my reality. I was never a religious person since my family was not really involved in it.

So, I grew up in a world with the notion that there was a big bang and that evolution, according to Darwin, is the way things were. What accompanies this western, Newtonian worldview is also a perception that we are separate from everyone around us, including people and the planet.

That's the root cause of suffering and why we are witnessing the destruction of Mother Earth.

We clearly must see it as separate from us to destroy it.

How would we destroy it if we were it?

Coming back to anxiety, I want to share a bit about my background story before presenting you with the solution to recovery. Yes, I will present to you everything you need to recover from anxiety within the pages of this book.

Before I had anxiety, I was a confident individual. Like everyone else, there were challenges in my life. My mother passed away when I was 16 years old, and I recall visiting her often in hospital as a child.

At some point in my life's journey, around the age of 14, I started occasionally drinking alcohol and smoking cigarettes. It felt cool to be different. At some point, I started hanging around the wrong people and eventually began smoking weed regularly. I was in constant trouble at school as I didn't give a damn about it. My classmates thought it was funny that I only appeared with a notebook and a pen in school. I literally never did homework, and my dad would receive weekly emails and calls from the school about how bad my behavior was.

Needless to say, I was kind of a rebel.

Looking back, I understand this quite well, as I never liked being told what to do, and fitting into rigid systems was against my nature. I love freedom, my friend.

As my mother's health declined, I started going off the rails increasingly, so my father decided to send me to a boarding school in Ireland. I only survived a couple of weeks there until I was kicked out. I ended up in another boarding school in Germany, where I managed to stay a bit longer until I got kicked out of there too. Then I ended up in a boarding school in Cologne, Germany, which I finally completed with decent grades.

It was here where things seemed to stabilize a bit in terms of my behavior. I also met my first girlfriend here, with whom I had a relationship for three years. I guess this was also quite stabilizing for me, this feminine love and energy.

Fast forward a couple of years, and upon my graduation from high school, I was admitted to a university in Aberdeen, Scotland. This was in 2012, and I remember my girlfriend broke up with me via text before I went there, which was a heartbreaking experience since I was in love with her.

I remember arriving in Scotland during freshers' week, where you just go partying all the time and take part in events organized by the university during the day. The intention is to get to know fellow students in order to settle in well during the first week of university. A beautiful thing, really. I had very little interest in other women and was slightly depressed as a result of the break-up.

It soon also dawned on me that what I had been studying, Economics and Finance, was fundamentally flawed. I realized that this subject was just made up of mental concepts with very little practical relevance in the actual reality.

It didn't help that I read a book called "Why I Left Goldman Sachs" by Greg Smith, which went behind the scenes into what one of the world's top investment banking firms is genuinely like. I learned that the financial industry was ultimately immoral and for sharks. This industry majorly contributed to the financial crisis in 2008 and the euro crisis, and it also relates to the mass inequality in our world.

My goal was to work there until I found out what it's actually like. Being an empathic person, I could not do something highly immoral. So, my life was seemingly breaking down.

I turned to drowning myself in alcohol and smoking weed, a habit I had kind of let go of when I got my high school graduation. It became an addiction again. My mission each day was getting weed. My best friend back then was amazed at my resourcefulness in somehow managing to obtain it, despite often not having the money.

There came a time where I truly noticed I was depressed. I was in a flat where some of my friends lived, and it suddenly dawned on me that my life was not fulfilling.

At some point, I started getting into even crazier drugs like MDMA, ecstasy, and LSD. Please don't do this as well! Luckily, that was only on a few occasions, and the one time it took LSD, I took way more than you're supposed to. I think I took four times (or more) the amount than you're supposed to. It was a crazy experience.

I recall looking at the TV, and the colors were coming out of it and swirling around the room. There was a sense of elation. My best friend was unsure whether or not he should do it, and I said, in a deep way, "You already know the answer." It felt like the universe was speaking through me and that I was the universe. There were yellow numbers everywhere; it was like I could see the code that makes up the cosmos. Needless to say, this was a mind-altering experience.

Before this experience, I remember that I had already started developing social anxiety, I guess because of smoking weed and avoidance tactics.

I was worried about my future because I no longer attended university. It has been programmed into my brain from a young age that I need to do that to be successful in life. So, I had a sense that my life was doomed.

Coming back to the LSD trip, it eventually ended badly and got overwhelming. I could no longer relate to the others in the room, and it felt like I had permanently lost touch with reality. I experienced an intense fear of never being able to return to normal.

Hours went by, and I eventually left the others in the living room and went into my bedroom, where I laid down and closed my eyes. I experienced fireworks exploding within me and intense spectacles of light.

While this might sound nice, it was terrifying. At some point, I returned to my normal sense of self and was grateful beyond measure. I thanked God for bringing me back to sanity.

The interesting thing is that I was no longer able to smoke weed from this day forward. What had become a way to self-medicate and suppress my pain now only caused intense anxiety.

By this time, it was very clear that I had developed social anxiety. The only thing that still "helped" me was drinking alcohol.

The winter holiday season had just arrived exactly after this experience, and I headed home to Germany to visit my dad. Shortly after, we went on holiday to Egypt, where it was very warm and sunny even in winter. This was somewhat of a family tradition back then.

There was one evening where I drank quite heavily at the hotel with other guests and the animation team. I remember the disco lights kind of flaring out at me, which caused me to freak out a bit. Eventually, I passed out drunk in my room.

The next morning was when all hell broke loose. I was panicking and freaking out. I thought I was going insane. It was at this moment that I developed full-blown anxiety. From that day forward, my life became radically different.

Ordinary, everyday things like socializing and leaving the house became a struggle. Even though I tried to get back into going to class and tutorials, it was very triggering, and my instincts told me to avoid it.

Over time, I completely isolated myself from society and became lonely beyond words. I felt like I was going insane and dropped into a dark hole. Depression was also a constant companion.

At some point, I got kicked out of university and lost my student funding. Money was slowly but surely running out. I remember there being only one option which was to get a job.

Luckily, I found a job rather quickly at the airport, working for a car rental company. The position I had was as a rental sales agent, where I sat at the desk in front of long queues of impatient travelers that had just gotten off their planes and were looking to pick up their car rentals.

This triggered my anxiety like crazy. I remember having a trembling voice and shaky hands as I spoke to the customers and entered their details into the computer for processing their car rental.

I also remember visiting this girl I knew in Spain shortly after being diagnosed with anxiety. In the past, we had quite a strong connection. She knew me as the old version before anxiety, where I was confident and happy.

I thought it might be a good idea to visit her in Madrid as a way to overcome anxiety. It was a strange experience because, when I met her, it was not the same as the last time. We met, went to a bar, and had a few drinks. I only had one as I knew that anxiety would otherwise make me feel terrible the next day.

We seemed to get along initially despite the circumstances. I stayed there for a couple of days, and at some point, she became a bit frustrated with me and told me that I had changed and left crying. She had seemingly noticed how I had changed. I was ok with the fact that she left because she had also changed somehow.

Shortly after this experience, and due to this immense, incessant pain within me, I eventually became obsessed with reading non-fiction books. I must have read hundreds of self-help books. It was quite encouraging to hear inspirational words and how people managed to transcend their challenges on a daily basis. This gave me a sense of hope on my journey.

It took me a while to figure out how to recover from anxiety naturally and permanently, which is what I am sharing with you in this book. I hope you're ready.

Thanks again for purchasing my book! I am confident that it will serve you well on your anxiety recovery journey.

In the next chapter, we will explore the common anxiety symptoms that make us think that we have some major illness or that something must be terribly wrong.

1. ANXIETY SYMPTOMS

Before talking about anxiety symptoms, I would like to mention the different forms anxiety takes.

There is generalized anxiety disorder (GAD), obsessive-compulsive disorder (OCD), post-traumatic stress disorder (PTSD), social anxiety, separation anxiety, panic disorder, and also different types of phobias such as health anxiety and agoraphobia. Depression is also a symptom associated with all these forms of anxiety.

In my experience, all of these are interrelated, and the way to recover is the same for all of the different forms that anxiety takes.

In the introduction, I talked about the Newtonian paradigm, which views us as separate from everyone else and also separates the body into different areas. That's why, in medicine, there are different branches for different types of issues. There appears to be an awareness of the role of emotions and trauma with respect to illness in our system, but it has not yet become mainstream.

Max Planck, a German theoretical physicist, said that "a new scientific truth does not triumph by convincing its opponents and making them see the light, but rather because its opponents eventually die, and a new generation grows up that is familiar with it."

A new branch of medicine has also emerged called functional medicine that looks at our body in a more holistic way. I never understood why hospital food was super unhealthy, for example, since what we eat has a huge effect on our health.

According to epigenetics, which is a relatively new field, it is our environment and lifestyle that affect gene expression. While everyone has probably got some bad genes that could potentially lead to illness, we are not solely at the mercy of our genes because our environment and lifestyle affect whether the bad genes are activated or not.

The keys here are environment and lifestyle. So, if we live next to a factory that produces harmful pollution, that can affect gene expression as our environment is unhealthy. In terms of lifestyle, what we eat and how we deal with our bodies has an effect on our gene expression and health too. The main argument I'm trying to make is that we have a powerful level of influence on our own health.

It's not fully clear what causes anxiety. I can only assume what caused mine, as mentioned in the introduction. What I know from personal experience is that anxiety is an accumulation of emotional blockages in the body's energy system.

Gary Craig, the founder of EFT, which is a powerful energy healing modality, says that "the cause of all negative emotions is a disruption in the body's energy system." I pretty much view it the same way. In some instances, I believe that it can be caused by diet as well. It could also be passed on from our environment, meaning family, parents, work, friends, partners, etc.

In self-help, there is this common idea and concept that we become the average of the five people we surround ourselves with. I've found this to be quite accurate in my life.

In the past, when I was going off the rails, I would hang out with the "wrong crowd," and I would become more and more similar to them. Over time, as my environment changed, I also changed. This even ties into the idea of epigenetics that I mentioned above.

Anxiety or a phobia can also be caused by a specific traumatic event, a series of events, or just a gradual accumulation of stress throughout life. It could also be caused by taking drugs. For example, many people with anxiety got it from smoking weed.

What I discovered is that we don't necessarily have to know or find the exact route cause of anxiety to recover from it. My intention is to show you that there can be varying causes, but the essence of anxiety is usually an emotional disruption in the body's energy system.

It's quite common to think you are going insane when you have anxiety. When I had it, I feared I was going crazy and becoming psychotic or developing schizophrenia. But the difference between someone that is sane and someone that is crazy is that they are unaware of their insanity. Just think of the person that walks down the road speaking to themselves. They are unaware of it. But you are aware of anxiety and its craziness. Therefore you are sane.

Eckhart Tolle put this beautifully in his book "A New Earth," where he wrote, "to recognize one's own insanity is, of course, the arising of sanity, the beginning of healing and transcendence."

It is not surprising that there are so many people in the world who are suffering from anxiety and depression. We are born into this world relatively free. You only have to observe the intense degree of presence within babies to observe their freedom. They have not yet been socialized, traumatized, or gone through our education system.

> *"It is no measure of health to be well adjusted to a profoundly sick society."*
> *Jiddu Krishnamurti*

It's pretty obvious how dysfunctional our society is. This also ties into the Newtonian paradigm of separation because we view ourselves as separate and seek to enhance this ego-sense. In extreme cases, this leads to war and other destructive tendencies. Love seeks to unite, heal and grow, whereas ego seeks to divide and destroy.

As we enter this world relatively free, we feel at one with life since we don't have an ego or identity yet. Then we get a name and are told that we are a person and taught that certain things are good and bad. As we grow up, we are punished, told to be quiet, and fit in.

The underlying message is that we are not good enough and acceptable. It's like a never-ending cycle of projection and social conditioning. It gets passed on from generation to generation. Many of our beliefs are not our own but society's beliefs.

There's a book called "Reality Transurfing" by Vadim Zeland that talks about a concept called pendulums. Pendulums are units or entities of collective thought energy. Pendulums follow their own agenda, often to the detriment of the individual that is feeding them. Pendulums can be people, organizations, companies, groups, or nations.

In Germany, it's common to watch the news at 8 pm every day. Collectively, millions of people are attuning their thoughts to the news and how terrible the world is. That's why I quit watching the news during my recovery, as I understood that emotional freedom and the news are mutually exclusive. I believe the news is one of the most destructive pendulums contributing to humanity being stuck in a vibration of fear and anxiety. It's not necessary to watch the news because people will tell you what is happening anyway. My life has been so much more peaceful since quitting the news years ago, and I can notice a clear difference between those who follow it and those who don't.

Our society is like the Matrix, which is why Keanu Reeves said, "The truth is, the Matrix was a documentary." We are truly a product of our environment. In that sense, it's not our fault that we now have this situation called anxiety.

In terms of anxiety symptoms, there are quite a few. The list below is by no means final.

- Intrusive thoughts
- Numb chest
- Difficulty breathing
- Heart palpitations
- Chest Tightness
- Pain in the chest
- Depersonalization/Derealization
- Difficulty with eye contact
- Panic attacks
- Brain fog
- Feeling disoriented
- Dizziness
- Shaking
- Shortness of breath
- Feeling detached from the real world
- Restless legs and arms
- Low energy
- Insomnia
- Sweating
- Feeling of having a heart attack
- Headaches

- Severe head, shoulder, and neck tension
- Tight jaw and, or, clenching teeth
- Fear of going insane
- Feeling dizzy
- Head and neck shakes
- Feeling afraid
- Feeling fear
- Feeling nervous
- Feeling scared
- Feeling sad
- Feeling down
- Feeling of impending danger or doom
- Feeling petrified
- Feeling restless
- Feeling tense
- Feeling weak
- Feeling tired
- Overthinking/analyzing
- Hard to relax or get comfortable
- Wanting to escape a situation
- Trying to stay in control
- Backaches
- Fear of doing things you enjoy
- Anger and frustration
- Tingling in the body
- Stories on loop
- Lack of focus
- Numbness
- Blurred vision and floaters
- Hot and cold flashes

- Difficulty breathing
- Hyperventilating
- Increased heart rate
- Trembling
- Troubles with digestion
- Music playing in your head, which is a form of OCD
- Memory loss

In general, the reason we experience emotions like fear or anxiety is for our survival. For most of our evolutionary history, we have been hunter-gatherers. Back then, we were constantly exposed to danger and threat, which is why we have these emotions and the fight-or-flight response. What has been a useful aid in our evolution has now become a hindrance to emotional freedom.

As a result of our upbringing and life experience, we have accumulated a significant amount of emotional pain, which manifests as anxiety. One of the strangest symptoms is depersonalization or derealization, where you feel emotionally numb and disconnected - almost like you are not even human. It can be like a void that causes anxiety, too, because it feels as though something is amiss.

The issue with anxiety symptoms is that they are so intense and convincing. They make you feel like something majorly wrong is happening. There are so many symptoms because your energy system has become unbalanced and stuck in fight-or-flight mode. When the fight-or-flight response is activated, the body essentially behaves as if it is in a survival situation. That's why you have weird, crazy, irrational thoughts and feel this sense of impending doom.

As energy is being directed towards opting between fight-or-flight, there are issues with memory and not knowing what to say, as these are not essential in a survival situation. You may also experience blurry vision and floaters as a result of the fight-or-flight reflex. All these symptoms are just created by anxiety and usually fade away as you recover. However, it's important to get checked by the doctor to rule out any other causes.

Once you've done that, you can rest assured that it's just anxiety and focus on recovery by following the principles in this book.

2. THE TRUTH ABOUT ANXIETY

"All truth passes through three stages. First, it is ridiculed. Second, it is violently opposed. Third, it is accepted as being self-evident."
Arthur Schopenhauer

I remember coming back to Scotland after the holiday in Egypt that initiated my anxiety disorder. It got so bad that I asked my dad to come over and stay with me.

After he came over, I decided to go to the doctor, or GP as they are called in the UK. I remember sitting in front of the doctor, who was a skinny, friendly, Scottish man with grey hair.
After a brief examination and me describing my symptoms, he told me it's most likely anxiety and that I would have it for the rest of my life. I was then prescribed some heart rate-reducing pills for the time being.

I don't know about you, but for me, that was a terrible experience. And I've heard from others who have had anxiety that they've been told the same.

One of the cognitive biases of our brain is called *authority bias*, which is the tendency to give greater weight to the opinion of authority figures. It's tragic that authority figures are stating it is not possible to recover because our beliefs create our reality. You see, everything in our reality is a reflection of our beliefs, thoughts, emotions, and actions. Beliefs are just thoughts that we have repeated regularly and are now ingrained.

Hebb's rule states, 'Neurons that fire together, wire together.'[1] We literally have these neural pathways that strengthen as a result of our repetitive thinking.

Take a moment to look around you and observe your surroundings. In order to exist, every object was first imagined in someone's mind and then created. If we think or believe that we can create or do something, we will do it. Henry Ford famously said, "Whether you think you can, or you think you can't - you're right." The subconscious cannot distinguish between what is real and what is vividly imagined.

For example, if I tell you **not** to think of a pink tiger, you still get that image in your mind.

The fewer limiting beliefs we have, the more likely we are to act on our intuition, inspiration, and

---

[1] Calbet, J. (2018). *Hebb's rule with an analogy. Psychology and neuroscience.* [online] NeuroQuotient. Available at: https://neuroquotient.com/en/pshychology-and-neuroscience-hebb-principle-rule/.

imagination. Everything we can imagine is potentially real, and the only limits are the ones we set for ourselves. See how everything is a reflection of that which is within. That's why Jesus said that the kingdom of heaven is within you. Heaven is not a place but a state of consciousness we can realize that is a condition of peace, love, and joy.

The truth is that we can recover from anxiety. I am living proof, and there are many stories of others that have managed to recover as well. I've also personally helped others recover. I'm not asking you to believe me. I want you to verify it for yourself by applying what you are learning here in your life.

Wim Hof says that "feeling is understanding," which means that we don't have to wait for science or depend on it to know the truth. We can try something, see how we feel, and find out the truth that way.

I remember telling a friend about a powerful breathing technique, but he didn't want to try it because there was no science behind it. However, it's quite clear when doing it that you feel amazing. In my opinion, feeling good is the ultimate truth because science comes from the mind.

Remember the Newtonian view that dominates scientific thought I mentioned in the introduction?

There is a deeper dimension beyond thought and science: our true nature, also known as awareness, presence, or consciousness.

As mentioned above, anxiety is just an accumulation of blocked emotions in the body's energy system. When we address this accumulation in the right way, we start recovering.

One anxiety symptom that really freaked me out was blurry vision and floaters. It reached a point where I went to an eye doctor and got my eyes tested. After doing the test, he told me I had great vision. That further confirmed to me that what I had was just anxiety.

That's why I recommend going to the doctor if you believe there is an underlying condition to rule it out so you can rest knowing that it's just anxiety.

One of the common questions is, "Does this ever get better?" I can tell you that, yes, it does get better over time. All the crazy symptoms listed above disappear as you recover from anxiety. I used to have them all, and now I have zero of them. In fact, my life has become better than before I had anxiety. In that sense, I am grateful for the experience of anxiety.

When faced with adversity, we have two choices:

1. Give up
2. Decide to find a way

I'm not sure why, but I decided to go with option number 2, and I encourage you to do the same.

When the doctor told me I would not recover, I was like, "Screw that; I'm finding my own way." I only took the pills I was prescribed for a couple of days and then decided to go natural. I went to free counseling offered by the university, but that seemed like a waste of time since the counselor was just listening to me and seemed clueless. I believe that many professionals don't really know what they are doing.

The key to success in any endeavor is a concept called *modeling* that comes from NLP, which stands for Neuro-Linguistic Programming. Modeling basically means finding someone with the results you want and copying what they are doing or have done. That's why I invested a lot of time in reading, investing, and working on myself because I understood that the way I've been doing things led me to where I am today. I was studying others that managed to transcend their challenges and live happy lives.

3. MEDICATION

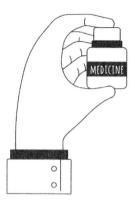

Medication can be useful in the beginning, especially when it's overwhelming and hard to function normally. But there comes a point in your recovery journey where it's best to let it go.

Medication can have a lot of undesirable side effects, and I've never been a fan of it. Whenever I am sick or have a headache, I don't take a pill but rather allow my own immune system to work it out. I understand that everyone is different, and for some of us, it makes sense to take medication.

It's never black or white, and I also don't know you personally, so what I am writing here is my general philosophy. I'm also not a doctor, so this does not constitute medical advice.

What I do know, however, is that truly we are powerful beyond measure.

Remember the point about epigenetics earlier? Our lifestyle and environment determine our health. Those are things that are within our control.

During anxiety recovery, I read hundreds of books about all kinds of topics. I self-educated and made many interesting discoveries about life. I read a lot of books about health and what is clear to me is that our system is broken. Just look at the recommended "healthy" diet. It has nothing to do with health. A healthy diet is something completely different. Anyway, I'll be getting into diets later in the book.

My recommendation would be to find more holistic professionals because when addressing the body and mind in this way, we can often stop taking medication. Please don't just radically stop taking any medication but rather taper off it slowly and discuss it with your doctor. Even if it's a mainstream doctor, you can tell them how you're doing all these things that will reduce your need for it. Sooner or later, you will reach a point in your recovery where it makes sense to taper off and eventually quit medication.

4. THOUGHT, EMOTION & AWARENESS

"Everything in life is vibration."
Albert Einstein

We live in a vibrational universe, where everything vibrates at different frequencies. That's why Nikola Tesla said, "If you want to find the secrets of the universe, think in terms of energy, frequency, and vibration."

Matter makes up only a small percentage of reality. The vast majority is empty space, pure energy. Even in us, below our skin, our matter, our physical form is mostly empty space made up of energy that vibrates at a certain frequency. When we change our energy, we change our lives.

Below is an image of the Hawkins Scale of Consciousness.

On this scale, we can see different levels of consciousness or levels of energy that we can experience as human beings. The scale is logarithmic, meaning there's an exponential rather than a linear difference between these levels.

If we think of enlightened beings like Buddha, Sri Ramana Maharshi, and Jesus, they most likely operate at 700+ most of the time. They experience peace, love, joy, harmony, and being present in the moment. This is the kingdom of heaven, which I alluded to earlier as being a state of consciousness.

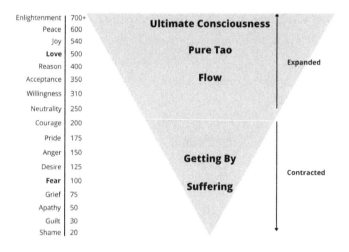

Fear or anxiety is at a level of 100, which is between suffering and getting by. It is a contracted state of being where we feel worried most of the time.

While this scale of consciousness looks static, we can experience varying states of consciousness throughout our daily lives. Even when you experience an anxiety disorder, there can be moments of peace in there. As we start letting go of our painful emotional baggage and start recovering from anxiety, we move up the scale of consciousness. When we start reaching the level of courage, we start moving into power vs. force. There is a greater sense of flow and empowerment and less heaviness and negativity.

In his book "Letting Go: The Pathway of Surrender," David Hawkins suggests moving up the scale of consciousness by using the mechanism of surrender. Essentially, this means allowing our emotional pain to be there as best as we can. It means to no longer resist our emotional pain and accept it.

The Latin derivative of emotion, 'emotare,' means energy in motion. Emotion is energy in motion. It just wants to be felt so it can leave the body. Eckhart Tolle also talks about this in his book "The Power of Now," as do many other spiritual teachings and self-help books.

During my anxiety recovery, I became obsessed with self-help and reading books. There was an intuitive knowing that there is a way out. The way out is the way in.

As we progress spiritually, the teachings unfold within us as experiential knowing rather than an intellectual understanding. It is then that we attain true wisdom. Even beyond anxiety recovery, there is much room to grow and evolve consciously and spiritually.

I have talked about the Newtonian paradigm that still dominates our thinking. It's this perception - we are separate individuals, separate from everyone and everything around us - that creates so much suffering within and outside of ourselves. Part of this accumulation of pain is our identification with it. We tend to view our thoughts and emotions as who we are.

But who is it that is aware of thought and emotion? To whom do these thoughts arise? If the answers to those questions lead to "me," we can further inquire, "Who am I?"

The purpose of these questions is not a mental answer but rather to realize our true nature. It's the realization that we are awareness, consciousness, the universe, or whatever name you want to use for it. In essence, we are all one, the same being.

Consciousness just is, and it is playing the game of creation of form to understand itself because it is formless. Its nature is pure love, hence why the highest consciousness states correspond to that as seen on the Hawkins scale above. That's also why that is heaven on earth where we realize our infinite divine nature.

As a result of this realization, the ego and our identification with thought and emotion lessen, increasingly allowing our true nature to shine through.

The challenge lies in the very ego that blocks this awareness. Literally, the truth has been rejected collectively for eons. For eons, humanity has been suffering.

Just look at what Jesus experienced. He was ahead of his time, and his message was too pure for the world, so they outright destroyed his body-mind or form identity. I'm sure he lives on as a being in the formless realms.

Talking about formless realms, it's rather interesting. As we raise our vibration and start moving up the scale of consciousness, we become more sensitive to life. We feel life more and experience it increasingly from a place of love and in a heart-centered way.

My mother passed away 12 years ago, and around a year ago, 11 years after her passing, she came to me as I was walking up the stairs at home. Even writing about this gives me chills because it was an experience beyond words. I didn't see her or hear her presence but rather just felt her there. She said, "Everything is good, Andy. You are on the right path." This was a profound experience for me, and I'm generally grateful for my mother, whom I remember as always showing and giving me love no matter what. Even on her worst days, where she was unable to talk and leave the bed, my appearance would make her smile. She showed me what love is in many ways. Something I only realize now as I love myself more.

One of the rules of Mother Earth appears to be free will. We generally seem to have the freedom to create our reality, whether that's consciously or subconsciously. For many of us, this is still subconscious and remains so until we reclaim our power.

Anxiety is a spiritual challenge since we are infinite spiritual beings having a temporary human experience. We generally forget that we are these powerful human beings.

Since we usually don't feel incentivized to transform when things are ok, we experience so much suffering until we eventually surrender when the pain becomes unbearable. Spiritual teacher Michael Beckwith says that "Pain pushes until the vision pulls." In that sense, anxiety is a spiritual challenge by our higher self.

It's a lesson in letting go, surrender, and acceptance because that is the only way to truly heal it. In martial arts, there is this concept of using the opponent's force instead of resisting that force.
Because resistance literally empowers it.

Bruce Lee said, "Be like water." Just live in the flow, in tune with the vibration of nature. We can learn a lot from being in nature.

Notice how the trees look like our lungs. We breath in what they breath out and vice versa. Everything is one.

5. LESSONS FROM PERSONAL EXPERIENCE

"I truly believe that everything that we do and everyone that we meet is put in our path for a purpose. There are no accidents; we're all teachers - if we're willing to pay attention to the lessons we learn, trust our positive instincts and not be afraid to take risks or wait for some miracle to come knocking at our door."
Marla Gibbs

During my recovery, there was a lot of pain to feel and experience. It seemed like a never-ending flow of anxiety, depression, fear, pain, doubt, and all the crazy symptoms associated with it.

The idea of surrender was first introduced to me by Paul David's book "At Last a Life," which is a great book on overcoming anxiety. It literally came to me in one of the darkest periods of my life when I was still living in Scotland. I had to reread it a bunch of times because it wasn't easy to practice acceptance in the midst of anxiety as it was so overwhelming.

One of the challenges with anxiety is that you tend to think it's something else, so you might find yourself frequenting forums, researching anxiety, and obsessing about it. This actually maintains the condition. You definitely want to go to the doctor and get checked. Once you do that and know it's just anxiety, the key is to no longer research it and focus on recovery instead.

What I also discovered was this idea of facing our fears. Anxiety is like a prison. It tells us that we must stay at home, that we are going insane, and that we cannot do what we used to do or the things we enjoy.

I talked earlier about how our beliefs create our reality. Can you see how anxiety is creating this limiting reality? But anxiety is not who we are in essence. So, the key is to do the things we are afraid of anyway, even if they freak us out.

As mentioned, I had to get that job at the airport, where I was majorly exposed to people, which triggered my social anxiety a lot. In a way, that was great because I had to face my fears head-on. Thank you, Universe, for that experience.

When you discover that acceptance and facing your fear is the key to anxiety recovery, it's liberating. All you have to do is surrender and face fear.

Why is facing fear important? Because by facing fear, remaining in that situation, and surrendering to it, we are sending a powerful message to our subconscious.

We are teaching it that we no longer need anxiety. We are deleting this unnecessary program. Through repeated exposure and eventually calming down in those situations that will happen at some point, we are rewiring our brain to be normal again and respond to our environment healthily and naturally.

Now, the key to this approach is patience. You need to stop trying to get better or get rid of anxiety or wanting it to be different because that is a form of resistance that literally enhances it. It took a while to come, so it will take a while to leave. It's like a pot of boiling water with a lid on it. When we resist our feelings and thoughts, they start bubbling up and eventually overflow. When we surrender, we remove the lid so the steam can leave naturally.

Emotion is energy in motion. It just wants to be felt so it can leave the body. Feeling is healing. The recovery process takes time. Of course, you can accelerate it in certain ways, but the essence is to surrender and feel it. It's that simple. When anxiety is here, that's ok; it's like a little baby or child that needs loving attention.

Eventually, I moved back to Germany. It felt right to leave Scotland and start anew. In Germany, I attempted to study again, or let's say my dad tried to persuade and force me. When I had enrolled again, it still seemed utterly pointless, so I eventually left it.

In the previous job situation in Scotland, I had a boss that was being totally mean and unfair to me. It got to the point where I asked him to go outside with me, where I told him, "If you keep treating me this way, we are going to have a problem." Whilst it did become a little better after that, the vibe was still off. I'm again thankful for this experience because it showed me that having a boss is not for me and that I prefer being self-employed. I'm a free spirit, my friend.

Just because we surrender, it does not mean we have to stay in situations that are not in alignment with our highest good. Surrender gives us the ultimate place from which to make the right decisions.

Reading a lot of self-help books massively helped to rewire my brain. They talked about how we can do amazing things, that we all have a unique vision, mission, and purpose and that we can overcome our limitations. As a result of reading, I became inspired to become self-employed. This option seemed way more appealing to me than going to a job with a boss that tells me what to do. By the way, I'm not suggesting that you need to quit your job and that becoming self-employed or doing that is better than a job; I'm just referring to my individual preference.

There are people who love and enjoy their job, and that is great. I would highly recommend finding a passion, hobby, or creative pursuit you can engage in to take your mind off things, so you no longer obsess about anxiety. You want to be busy, accept that anxiety exists in the background, and live normally, as best as you can.

As mentioned earlier, one of the principles of personal growth is modeling, so I decided to model other people that were self-employed. So, I read books about it and invested in training and coaching. I joined a business mastermind that cost me a couple of thousand dollars, which was money I did not have at that time.

After saving up for five months, I decided to join the program. Part of me was hugely skeptical about this investment, but another part of me just thought of it as an investment that could work out or not. I adopted this mentality of being an investor in myself.

When I joined this program, I was added to a group with around 200 entrepreneurs. A few were millionaires, and it was normal for them to run a 6-figure business. To me, this was crazy and completely outside of my reality. There were constant posts being made nearly every day about someone closing a new sale for a thousand dollars or more. The business model was a social media marketing agency where you deliver a service in exchange for money to businesses. You manage their social media ads, and they pay you in return. It's a win-win situation, so they happily pay you money.

After five weeks of being in the program, I closed a sale for 500 dollars, which was a mind-blowing experience. This permanently shifted my reality and showed me it was possible. The crazy thing is that I did all this while I had anxiety and the symptoms. I understood that the more I did the uncomfortable, the more comfortable I would become.

Eventually, I even started cold calling companies, which means calling them without them knowing you to arrange a meeting with the intent of doing business. That triggered a lot of fear, and there was a lot of pain from being rejected. I knew that surrender and facing fear was key. They became my new source of strength and empowerment.

On the next page there is an image from a Facebook message my buddy Dean sent me, who is on the path to recovery. His message contains the essential anxiety recovery principles.

Not complacent mate
.but I'm recovering .alot
of fear going away I
actually even feel now
its not such a big deal.if
it comes on ..yes the odd
days it's there setbacks
..But .I'm so glad I got
this far ......the answer is
not to be scared of it
..invite it . And face the
fears ....etc excersise.eat
right .cut down on
caffeine..stay busy...talk
to others. ...D great !!!!!!

 1

Along my journey, I also got into doing things like
meditation and morning routines, etc., but I will talk
more in-depth about that later.

I want to make a key point here that this is not about
being perfect. There were many setbacks on my
journey, and I felt a lot of fear in those scary.
situations. Sometimes I didn't face fear and just stayed
at home when I had a really bad day.

Setbacks are 100% normal and to be expected during anxiety recovery. They are actually a sign of progress and also to be accepted. This, too, shall pass.

I remember a slightly embarrassing story.

The area where I live in Germany is a wine-producing region, and in summer, they have these wine feasts with food and wine stands and music where people from the villages meet up and socialize. Some friends invited me to go, and I went anyway because I knew I had to leave the house to recover.

I ended up being on the dance floor, and there was this woman that seemed to be interested in me and dancing next to me. I kind of freaked out because of anxiety, left, and went home. The next day my friends asked me where I had disappeared to, and I just said that I didn't feel well.

So, it's ok not to be perfect. I never was. Sometimes I ate some crappy food or fell back into old habits and patterns. That's ok. Perfection is an illusion and most likely just another program we have inherited from our society.

If you find it challenging to fall asleep at night, you could listen to some nature sounds, guided meditations for sleep, or focus on your breath to fall asleep. Remember that you can also download my

FREE Guided Meditation For Anxiety Relief by visiting andykloss.com/book-gift.

I often just focused on my breath to fall asleep. In hindsight, I now know that the breath is a powerful tool for anchoring yourself in the present moment, which I will share more about later on in the book.

"Conscious breathing heightens awareness and deepens relaxation."
Dan Brule

6. THE ANXIETY DIET

The Anxiety Diet, oh my, this is a controversial area, isn't it?

We are all unique beings with different bodies. So, I don't believe in a one size fits all approach.
That being said, there are definite principles we can follow to ensure that we are healthy human beings.

Earlier, I talked about epigenetics, which means that our lifestyle and environment affect our gene expression and health. Diet is a huge component of lifestyle and thus affects our health in a major way. For some of us, anxiety could also be caused by elements of our diets, especially sugar. Therefore, it makes sense to eat healthier.

One of the definite principles of healthy nutrition is eating whole foods. This means eating foods that are not processed and don't contain any additives or chemicals. Trans fat is particularly unhealthy for us and is found in way more products than you might think.

The key is to turn around the product packaging, ignore the marketing and look at the actual ingredients. Ingredients are listed in order of how much they are contained. So the first thing that appears makes up most of the item and, vice versa, the last least. Ideally, there should only be whole actual foods on that list, not chemicals, additives, or colorings: nothing that did not come naturally from Mother Earth.

What is also clear is that eating mostly plants is the way to go. Greens, salads, fruits, and vegetables in varying colors. I personally don't eat eggs, meat, or fish, but if you desire to do so, I would try and get it from natural, free-range, or organic sources if possible. With fish, you want to avoid aquaculture as this is very unhealthy. Natural, from the sea, is the best.

I recovered from anxiety eating eggs, meat, and fish and couldn't always afford the healthiest options, so it's not necessary to quit those things. I also didn't eat perfectly all of the time. That being said, I did ensure that I was generally eating healthy. It has been a more recent, intuitive decision, post overcoming anxiety to eat in a vegetarian way.

In terms of oils, I would recommend using extra virgin olive oil and coconut oil. Many of the common oils we use have the wrong omega-6 and omega-3 ratios. Also, when frying, make sure the oil never starts smoking as it then becomes toxic.

Everyone is unique and individual in this area, so it's key to find what works for you. Doing a blood test with the doctor and checking deficiencies makes sense too. For example, maybe you need vitamin D3 supplementation if you don't get enough sun. It's best to check for any underlying causes and rule them out. Just be careful when listening to the mainstream diet recommendations because they are not really healthy.

There are many great resources out there.

Here are some books on nutrition that helped me improve my health:

- "Eat Fat Get Thin" by Dr Mark Hyman (Paleo Diet)
- "Becoming Vegan" by Brenda Davis (Vegan Diet)
- "The Detox Miracle" Sourcebook by Robert Morse (Raw Food & Detoxing)

I would also like to recommend two documentaries on Netflix at this stage. I think it's important that we become aware of the fact that our excessive consumption of animal products is one of the main ways in which we are destroying the planet. It is also the greatest contributor to climate change, not to mention the mass cruelty and suffering these sentient animals experience. The two documentaries are *Seaspiracy* and *Cowspiracy*.

It's truly devastating what kind of impact we are having, and the way we are living is not sustainable. The key to transformation is awareness. So I'm choosing a vegetarian or plant-based diet for our planet and Mother Gaia.

If you choose to eat animal products, I would highly recommend getting them locally from a farm where the animals are treated well and have a good and happy life. Go for quality vs. quantity. Less is more.

I personally believe that when we consume factory-farmed stuff where they are treated inhumanely, we then consume that fear energy stored within the flesh of these sentient beings. When I went vegetarian, I noticed a huge difference in my energy levels, so it might be worth checking out for yourself.

If coffee triggers your anxiety too much, it might be worth reducing or quitting it for the time being. You could try coffee without caffeine or even opt for a healthier alternative like green tea. Green tea is great because it contains an amino acid called l-theanine that actually reduces anxiety and has numerous other health benefits.

I would also recommend getting enough magnesium in your diet. Magnesium is proven to reduce anxiety. Foods that are high in magnesium include dark chocolate, nuts and seeds, avocados, legumes, tofu, fatty fish, bananas, and leafy greens.

It's best to get your vitamins and nutrients from natural sources instead of supplements. Make sure that you are also getting enough omega-3 in your diet. The only supplements I would recommend are maybe vitamin B12 if you are vegetarian or plant-based and vitamin D3 if you live in the northern hemisphere. If you supplement, make sure it's as natural as possible. Nature is the greatest healer.

There is an amazing healing tool I use regularly. I learned it from Dr. Mark Hyman, and it is called an *Ultra Bath*.

- Add two cups of Epsom salt (475 grams), half a cup of baking soda (90g), and ten drops of lavender oil to a hot bath and soak in it for 20 minutes.

The Epsom salt is high in magnesium which reduces anxiety, while the lavender oil helps you relax. It's great to do this in the evening before going to sleep. The baking soda also alkalizes your body and water, which is great because the standard diet we eat is very acidic.

"No disease can exist, including cancer, in an alkaline environment."
Dr. Otto Warburg

By adding the Ultra Bath to your toolbox, you are detoxing your body, alkalizing your body, and reducing stress and anxiety. I personally believe that the Ultra Bath also has an effect on a more spiritual level in cleansing the aura and removing negative vibrations. It's like a total reset for the body.

7. PATIENCE IS A VIRTUE

"Patience attracts happiness; it brings near that which is far."
Swahili Proverb

I remember that my mother would always tell me that patience is a virtue.

According to the Cambridge dictionary, a virtue is "a good moral quality in a person, or the general quality of being morally good." Patience is "the ability to wait, or to continue doing something despite difficulties, or to suffer without complaining or being annoyed."

It's evident that patience is key during anxiety recovery because it has the very qualities that align with the art of surrender, acceptance, allowing, welcoming, and letting go. These are all words that describe the same thing in essence.

When we are impatient, we want things to be different *now*. The consequence is that we reject anything that is not desirable and resist it. We judge, disown and suppress it. It then becomes stored in our body as our shadow self.

We think that when we are feeling anxious that it's bad, and we should not feel this way. In other words, we are impatient with ourselves. It is this very impatience or resistance that keeps anxiety alive. That's why some of us have suffered for years or decades. It is the degree to which we resist that we suffer.

Our shadow self, which is our suppressed emotional pain, the ego, which manifests as anxiety and depression, therefore remains stored within us until we are willing to face it with patience and acceptance. When we shine the light of awareness onto our pain, we are dissolving it.

Because it took a while for anxiety to come, it can take a while to leave. That's why patience is key which simply means to allow recovery to take as long as it needs. This very inner attitude, ironically, will accelerate the healing process. It's counterintuitive in that sense.

You might be wondering how long the recovery process takes. There is no definite answer to this question, and it depends on the extent to which you implement the recovery principles in this book.

What I can tell you is that if you follow the principles, you will recover, and you will notice the change.

8. SADHANA

Sadhana is the Sanskrit word for spiritual practice. Since we are spiritual beings having a human experience, spiritual practice is a way to reconnect to our true nature and reduce suffering.

The highest state of being is enlightenment, the end of suffering. This is level 700+ on the Hawkins Scale. These are just different levels of consciousness, and no human is better than another.

Similarly, an old person is not better than a young person. Herein lies also the danger of the spiritual ego, which manifests as seeing oneself above others who have not yet reached the same level. In essence, we are all one being manifested in different forms, so it doesn't really matter.

While sadhana can refer to a dedicated time where we sit down and practice something like meditation, our entire life experience is a form of spiritual practice. This is because transcending anxiety and our shadow is an ongoing process arising in each moment as the pain surfaces from the subconscious.

The practice for this is surrender. That is the foundational, number one practice to implement on this journey whenever any discomfort arises. There are quite a few other forms of spiritual practice that are highly valuable. Some of the main ones I have practiced are meditation, breathwork or pranayama, EFT, the Wim Hof Method, morning routines, the law of attraction, visualization, affirmations, and journaling.

Meditation

Let's talk about meditation. While there are many meditation techniques, the essence of meditation is always the same. Meditation is a practice we commit to for a certain time period each day. It's usually wise to start with only a few minutes a day to build the habit. When we start with 20 minutes from the get-go, it can become too much of a commitment, and we drop off.

I'm an intuitive person, so I would recommend going with the flow and your intuition with respect to the amount of time. However, if you are looking for guidelines, I would initially suggest doing anywhere from 1-5 minutes. Once you are at around 5 minutes, you can increase it intuitively in increments of 5 minutes, i.e., from 5 minutes to 10, from 10 to 15, from 15 to 20. I would do this in the morning when you wake up to start your day right. This is a way to automate your personal and spiritual growth.

There are many misconceptions about meditation. There is this idea that our mind has to be perfectly silent. That is not true. The objective of meditation is not to have a silent mind but rather to catch yourself being caught in thought. What happens when you sit down is that, at some point, you will realize that you have become lost in thoughts. When this happens, you gently refocus your awareness on your breath. This very process of constantly catching yourself being lost in thought and refocusing your awareness is the key.

Over time, this makes you more present to the moment and reduces thought activity. In just a few minutes a day, you can change the whole trajectory of your life.

Sadhana is a practice, so it's key not to have any expectations. Some sessions will be calm, while others may be hectic with lots of thoughts. The hectic sessions can be way more beneficial than the calm ones as here we are really training ourselves properly to be more present. It's like a muscle that is getting trained over time. It's key to ignore the short-term results, just like during anxiety recovery.

See how this is all about being in the flow with what is? That is true freedom. So, when thoughts arise during meditation, see them like clouds passing by in the sky. And as you become aware of being lost in thought, gently refocus on the breath. If there are a lot of negative emotions, the key is to really allow them to be there.

We are not refocusing our awareness onto our breath but rather onto the very emotions that are felt within our bodies. It's the same with physical pain; welcome and allow it to be there as best as you can. In that very moment, we are creating an inner sanctuary, an inner healing space. We are shining the light of awareness onto our pain. Darkness cannot survive in the light.

See how this ties in with the general practice of surrender throughout the day? It actually enhances our ability to surrender, i.e., makes us more present in daily life.

To recap, when we get lost in thought, gently refocus on the breath. When there are negative emotions, welcome them, allow them to be there, let them run their course. After they have passed, gently refocus on the breath. The key here is being gentle since we are dealing with self-love and our inner beingness.

I would suggest having a stopwatch or clock in front of you. I would not recommend using an alarm as this can shock you out of meditation. Just intuitively check your clock by opening one eye slightly.

For every 5 minutes of meditation, take at least 1 minute to come back to reality. When you are done, slowly move your fingers and toes, maybe stretch a bit, gently open your eyes and take your time to come back, especially if there is a sense of urgency to get up and get things done.

Patience is key. Beingness. Here. Now.

In terms of seating position, the most important thing is to have a straight spine. It does not have to be perfectly straight, and you do not have to force yourself into some kind of intense posture. You can either sit normally on a chair or cross-legged on a meditation cushion. The most important thing is that you are fully comfortable so you can focus on meditation. If there an ache or itch in your body during meditation, just move a bit or scratch it while keeping your eyes closed. When doing meditation, keep your eyes closed.

Morning Routines

According to University College London, it takes 66 days to change our habits. Everything we do is habitual. That's essentially how the brain and body work. They automate things. Even right now, you have a morning routine. Maybe you wake up, hit snooze, check your phone, have some water, make a coffee, and shower. Whatever you do, it is most likely habitual. So, the key is to use some willpower to establish this new habit in the morning.

Remember, it takes 66 days to form a new habit, so willpower is only required short-term. It's like a short-term sacrifice for a long-term reward.

Morning routines were a huge part of my journey. I experimented with all kinds of morning routines. What I found to work the best is just jumping out of bed even if you don't feel like it, having a glass of water, and brushing your teeth. This gets you up and out of bed.

When we are waking up, it's like our bodies are lying to us. Once we get up, we start feeling more awake. You can still go back to sleep after your morning routine if you are truly in need of rest. Listening to our intuition and the needs of our bodies is key.

It's ok to miss a day once in a while, but I would recommend being consistent with it. I was never perfect at this, but maybe you are a more consistent type of person than me. My personality type is an ENFP which means I dislike planning, routine, etc., and get bored with that easily. You can do a Myers-Briggs personality test online to learn more about your personality type as this raises self-awareness. You will likely learn a lot about yourself from doing this test.

After jumping out of bed, having a glass of water, and brushing your teeth, you have a few options. Generally, you want to start with some form of movement. This could just be some intuitive movement, stretching, or something like yoga or qigong. If you are looking for a specific routine, I would recommend either the 5 Tibetan Rites, which is a Tibetan Yoga routine, or The 8 Brocades of Qigong. Alternatively, it could be some other workout you like doing, such as going for a walk or a run. The key is to experiment, find what type of movement works for you, and integrate that into your routine. Maybe movement is not an option due to health reasons. That is perfectly fine too. You'd just not do that part of the morning routine.

Next up is breathwork, followed by meditation. I've shared a breathwork technique called Wim Hof breathing later on in the book that you can use. I would recommend committing to at least a few minutes of meditation in the morning.

After movement, breathwork, and meditation, you can add in some visualization. Visualization is most powerful after meditation. The subconscious mind cannot distinguish between what is real and that which is imagined. That is why we get sad when watching a sad movie. Really it's just pixels projected on a screen. So, by consciously visualizing what we want, we can retrain the subconscious mind.

In the Bible, it says, "Ask, and it shall be given you; seek, and ye shall find; knock, and it shall be opened unto you: For everyone that asketh receiveth; and he that seeketh findeth; and to him that knocketh it shall be opened." This is also known as the law of attraction, which states that like attracts like.

Everything we experience is a reflection of that which is within. Ask and it is given applies even if our asking is unconscious. The vibration we emit attracts to us our experience. In that sense, our reality is a mirror.

Can you see how when you have anxiety, the world is a scary place? Vice versa, people who are peaceful see the world as a peaceful place. The world is as we are being.

Collectively, we are waking up to this fact, and even you reading this is a part of that awakening. This very awakening process is creating a new heaven and earth, a new state of consciousness on this planet where the health of Mother Nature is restored, and we live as liberated human beings on earth in peace, love, joy, and harmony.

Coming back to visualization, it's key to focus not on what you don't want but rather on what you do. It's important that your vision is a beneficial one collectively. So, the vision is good for all, which includes your own well-being and profit.

Imagine your ideal life. Where would you be? What would you do? Where would you live? What career would you have? And your free time? Imagine, without limitation, what that would be like. Feel it, be it, this is your asking. But it comes from a place of being and having it already rather than wanting it due to lack.

If there is some discomfort visualizing, again, accept it. Never resist the emotions; always allow them to be there as best as you can.

As you finish your visualization, take a moment to be before doing the next practice.

By the way, you don't need to worry that you are manifesting negative things in your life because of anxiety, negative thoughts, and negative emotions. Simply welcome and accept them as this releases them over time. With thoughts, you also just allow them to be there. Alternatively, you can also welcome the feeling underlying a thought pattern.

Next, practicing gratitude is great for you. Write down in your journal or on a sheet of paper what you are grateful for, really feeling it. Make a list of at least five things you are grateful for. Make sure to switch it up, so it doesn't become repetitive over time. Maybe you don't think you have anything to be grateful for, but I can assure you that there are many things.

You could be grateful for reading this book, having a roof over your head, running tap water that can clean you, the sun shining outside, a nice, hot cup of tea that warms your soul, and much more. It's normal that you might not feel super grateful initially due to the momentum of the past, which is why it's a practice.

Over time, you will start to notice the benefits of feeling more grateful and happy in your life.

Here's a little practice session:

- Make sure you are undisturbed for the next few moments.
- Find a comfortable position sitting or lying down, close your eyes, and think about what you are grateful for.
- In case you are not feeling grateful, think of a positive moment from the past where you were truly grateful such as the day you passed your exams, or when you got an awesome Christmas present, or something else.
- Try and remember this feeling of gratitude; how did it feel for you? Cultivate the feeling and empower it, make it grow within your body, and transfer or implement this feeling to what you are grateful for today.

After gratitude, you could recite some positive affirmations. Here is a list of affirmations:

- Every day and every way, I am getting stronger and stronger.
- I easily accept my emotions and let go of them.
- I am a radiant expression of infinite potential.
- I manifest peace, love, joy, and harmony with ease.
- I am so grateful for my anxiety recovery.
- I love and accept myself as I am.
- I am beautiful. I am happy. I am free.
- I am powerful beyond measure.

- I am so happy that the universe or God is protecting me.
- I am radiantly healthy.
- I am peaceful and whole.
- I respect and love myself.
- I am so grateful to be living my passion and purpose.
- I nourish myself with high vibrational words and healing foods.
- I am connecting to my higher self.
- Abundance flows to me with ease.
- I am thankful for my life and all my experiences.
- I give myself space to grow and heal.
- The more I do the uncomfortable, the more I am comfortable.
- I am always on the right path.
- I am abundant and live in an abundant world.

You can create your own affirmations or find some online that inspire you. The key to manifestation is to focus on what you want to create, not what you don't want. These are just some ideas but only use affirmations that resonate with you. Of course, they might feel a bit unreal at first.

As you affirm, feel it, imagine it, be it, step into it. You can also create affirmations around certain goals that you have.

After practicing affirmations, you can read a non-fiction book that inspires you and gives you a sense of empowerment. Perhaps it feeds new ideas and concepts into your ecosystem, or maybe there is an online course or skill you are learning about. Something that helps you grow.

For me, reading is one of the fundamental things that will change your life. It's just so deep and profound.

We are the average of the five people we surround ourselves with. If our environment doesn't contain the right people, the best thing is just to read books to surround yourself with this new vibration.

My intention is for you to become the master of your life and empower you to find what works by guiding you in the right direction.

I would also recommend creating a vision board that has images and visual representations of what you'd like to manifest in your life over the next year. You can then look at it and imagine it throughout the day.

I would like to talk about two other spiritual tools I have found incredibly valuable, but I don't want to overwhelm you with all these new tools and practices. Less is more, initially, and then you can add more over time. If we try to do too many things at once, we may end up doing none.

As mentioned, it takes 66 days to build new habits, and there is only so much willpower each day. Every time we make a decision, talk to someone, watch something, or change our focus, we reduce our willpower to some extent. So, I don't want you to focus on too many things at once.

EFT Tapping

One of these spiritual tools is EFT, which stands for Emotional Freedom Techniques, sometimes referred to as tapping or EFT Tapping. It's an amazing healing modality that is like acupuncture without needles.

Based on the understanding of traditional Chinese medicine, we have these energy meridians that flow throughout our bodies. These meridians allow Qi, which is our life energy, to flow. In a healthy body, the energy flows and circulates naturally. When our health declines, there is usually a blockage of energy somewhere.

When there is a disruption in the body's energy system, for example, due to an overwhelming incident in our life experience, the energy cannot flow properly until we release the blockage. It's mind-blowing stuff.

In yoga, the meridian system is called *Nadi*, and it carries *prana*, life force, too. Different country, similar concept. These are ancient technologies that have so much more depth to them than our western approach.

Do you know why kids are so vital, vibrant, and alive? It's because the energy is still flowing, and they haven't been exposed to the craziness that is our world.

The beautiful thing is that we can work on making the energy flow again. We have the power.

In the system of EFT, there are certain meridian points that we can tap to release the blocked emotional energy. It works for negative emotions, thoughts, limiting beliefs, trauma, and even physical pain. Gary Craig, the founder of EFT, recommends trying it on anything.

In the following image, you can see the acupuncture points that EFT uses.

By tapping on each point with your index finger and middle finger held together and focusing on the issue you want to release, you can let go of the emotional disruption. We literally clear the issue from our energy bodies.

Remember the principle of patience. Inner work can take time, and it's key to just flow with it and have no expectations.

In the system of EFT, you choose an issue to focus on. This could be an emotion right now like anxiety, a situation at work that bothered you, something traumatic from the past, or even a physical symptom like a tight chest. **A word of caution here is that if it is a very traumatic incident, it may be wise to do EFT with an experienced practitioner.**

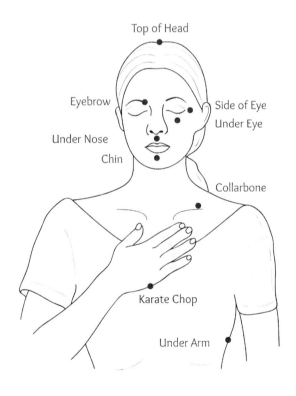

EFT Tapping Points

To get started, pick the issue you want to work on and assess the emotional intensity on a scale from 0-10. When you pick a number, it doesn't have to be perfect, just your best guess.

After you have picked your number, you start tapping.

As an example, I'm just going to use "anxiety" as the issue to work on. However, it could be an issue like "chest pain" or "when my parents hit me," or "I'm afraid to leave the house," as explained above.

So you have a set-up statement. The purpose of the set-up statement is to focus your awareness on the issue you want to let go of. In this example, we will use "anxiety."

Say three times, "Even though I have this anxiety, I deeply and completely love and accept myself," whilst tapping the Karate Chop point with your index finger and middle finger.

After you've done that three times, you use a remainder statement on the remaining points. You just say "this anxiety," or whatever issue you are working on.

The next point after the Karate Chop Point is the Top of Head Point. You just tap for approximately seven times or so while saying "this anxiety" once. You don't need to track the seven times as you will hit it anyway while saying the statement.

Then you tap on the eyebrow point around seven times, saying, "this anxiety."

Follow this with the side of eye point, under eye point, under nose point, chin point, collarbone point, under the arm point. Tap each of those around seven times while saying the remainder statement, "this anxiety," once for each tapping point.

That is one round of EFT.

You can stop after one round, close your eyes, breathe in deeply through your nose, and breathe out through your mouth. Now think of the issue you are working on, e,g, "anxiety," and assess the emotional intensity from 0-10. Maybe it went down, stayed the same, or went up. Either way, it's fine. Simply keep tapping until it goes down to zero or one.

At first, you are perhaps just removing the resistance to feeling, and it could go up, but whatever happens, all is well. It's just emotion, energy in motion, that wants to leave the body. As you tap, it may reveal other emotions or situations from the past that have been buried in the subconscious, or a physical problem. Then you just keep tapping on that. It's simple, really.

If the thing you are working on is super traumatic, it's important to be careful. If you were to imagine something highly traumatic, and I don't want you to go there right now, what would your level of intensity be? If that number is 50 or 100, it's key to do that with an experienced practitioner. Work on the little things first before going super deep. Get some experience with it.

The Wim Hof Method

The other tool that really helped me a lot was the *Wim Hof Method*. Wim Hof, "The Iceman," is quite an interesting guy. He is from the Netherlands and has 21 Guinness World Records, such as swimming below ice for 66 meters, running a full marathon in the Namib desert without water, and staying in a container with icy water for more than 112 minutes.

He has done a remarkable service for humanity by bringing ancient wisdom from the east to the west with his own unique spin on it. His message is that we can all become strong, happy, and healthy, rediscover our inner strength and that anyone can do what he can do.

As a result, he developed the Wim Hof Method, which is made up of 3 pillars:

- Cold Exposure
- Conscious Breathing (Breathwork)
- Commitment

Cold exposure is a very healthy thing as it boosts your metabolism, reduces inflammation and muscle soreness, improves sleep, strengthens the immune system, and reduces anxiety and depression.

Please be careful with practicing cold exposure if you have never done it before.

I've been practicing this method for a few years during the winter months here in Germany, and it has made a huge difference in my life. My personal ice bath record is 15 minutes in a frozen lake in the Vosges mountains in France. It's not necessary to do it in such an extreme way; even just ending the shower with 30 seconds of cold water can make a huge difference in how you feel.

When I learned the Wim Hof Method, I was still suffering from anxiety and desperately looking to get back to my old self. I was willing to try anything. I recall watching the VICE documentary[2] with Wim Hof on YouTube and it blew my mind. After doing some research, I decided to join is program and took action on it.

You start off gently with cold showers and then you transition to an ice bath. The message is that everyone can do it. You just have to be a bit careful if you have high blood pressure, for example.

Wim Hof says that 2 minutes of an ice bath is all you need to get the benefits, and it's way more powerful than cryotherapy. That being said, just taking cold showers is amazing as well for making you feel better.

Because this method changed my life, I decided to launch a local meet up group where I live in Freiburg, Germany. At the time of this writing there are 61 members in the group and a bunch of us meet up on the weekend to do the Wim Hof Method. It has been a huge blessing and has changed lives. I even met my amazing girlfriend Kateryna through this group which I am super grateful for.

In the following images you can see some actual ice bathing sessions from some of our excursions.

---

[2] YouTube. (2015). *The Superhuman World of Wim Hof: The Iceman.* [online] Available at: https://youtu.be/VaMjhwFE1Zw.

"When you go into the cold, you cannot think. You have to be. You learn to be… to be the best version of yourself."
Wim Hof

In the image above we managed to stay in frozen water for 10 minutes for the first time. It was a historic moment.

Conscious breathing or breathwork, also called *pranayama* in Yoga, is another powerful pillar. Wim Hof says that you can "get high on your own supply" using your breath to get you there.

The German word for breathing is *atmen* which comes from the Sanskrit word *Atman* which means spirit, soul, god, or our true self. By using our breath, we can go beyond the conditioning, ego, and pain into the depth of our being.

When practicing the breathing exercise, you start feeling tingly sensations in your body and might feel certain energies within. You might even see blue lights or stroboscope effects, but it's alright if that doesn't happen. The breathing might even lead to an emotional release in which pent-up emotions come up to leave the body. It's a beautiful thing, so the key is not to resist and just be with it.

Here is how to do the Wim Hof breathing technique. Please don't do this technique or any other strong breathwork technique during pregnancy or on a full stomach. Please do this breathing technique in a safe environment, like sitting on a couch or lying down on a yoga mat or bed as you might pass out. **Never perform the breathing technique whilst driving or in the water, as that could be fatal.**

Make sure you have an empty stomach.

Sit in a comfortable position on a chair or couch with a straight back, or lie down on a bed or yoga mattress so you are comfortable and your lungs can take in oxygen properly. I would suggest doing the Wim Hof breathing technique while lying down.

Take 30 to 40 deep breaths, fully into your belly, chest, and head, and let it out naturally, not forcing it out. Do this 30 to 40 times in a strong way. You might feel light-headed or feel tingly sensations; that's ok.

After your last exhale, hold your breath for as long as it feels right. You might be surprised at how long you can hold it. When you feel the need to breathe again, fully inhale and hold your breath for 10 to 15 seconds and then let it go.

That is one round of Wim Hof breathing. You can do 3 or 4 rounds. That's it.

It can be super powerful to do this, and you might feel amazing, but the key is not to have any expectations.

Then, go for a normal warm shower and turn it to cold for the last 30 seconds. When you enter the cold, make sure to focus your mind using the principle of mind over matter and maintain deep breathing. Override the instinctive shock and shiver response and stay calm in the cold. Accept it and surrender.

In order to warm up after cold exposure, do the horse stance as seen in the following image. You can move your arms from side to side across your body to warm up the body.

Next, you could go into meditation for 5-10 minutes. If you sometimes struggle with meditation, doing it now could make it a lot easier for you as you are calmer and more present. You can inhale through your mouth or nose.

That's the essence of the Wim Hof Method.

One of my biggest lessons from Wim Hof comes from his quote, "feeling is understanding." It doesn't matter what we think or what the science says. As we try something and see how we feel, we can learn the truth through our direct experience.

Breathwork

I would now like to talk about breathwork in general. The Wim Hof breathing technique is very similar to strong yogic breathing. In the system of yoga, breathwork is called *pranayama*. In Sanskrit, *prana* stands for breath or life force. *Yama* means control, and *ayama* means extend and expand. So pranayama is about extending and expanding life force energy through regulating your breath. That's why the Wim Hof breathing technique can make you get high on your own supply.

In Pranayama Yoga, there are strong and deep breathing techniques similar to Wim Hof breathing which activate and reset the mind and energy system. While the Wim Hof Method also encourages breathing through the mouth, in pranayama, it is recommended to do nasal breathing as the nose has important roles like filtering, warming, and moisturizing the air.

There are also other forms of breathing techniques like shamanic breathing. This is similar to Wim Hof breathing without retention for periods of 15, 20, 30 minutes, or even longer. And, you also have holotropic breathing, which goes even longer and is usually done in a setting with multiple people and a guide. Qigong also has breathing exercises and movements similar to yoga and pranayama.

You could also explore more gentle breathing practices such as box breathing where you inhale through the nose to a count of four, hold the air in for a count of four, exhale through the mouth to the count of four, hold your empty lungs to the count of four, and repeat for a few minutes. This can be helpful when you are on the go and don't have time for spiritual practice.

There are so many healing, life-affirming, and beautiful techniques and practices to explore. To me, it's mind-blowing that our society doesn't teach this. Part of the reason is that it is not profitable for the pharmaceutical industry that wants to sell drugs. It's also not in the interest of society to have people that are awakening to their true power.

Ho'oponopono

Another cool healing tool is *Ho'oponopono*, an ancient Hawaiian prayer that is as follows:
"I'm sorry, please forgive me, thank you, I love you."

You simply keep repeating the prayer until you feel better. It can also be used as a mantra during meditation. Instead of focusing on the breath as an object of meditation, you can do the Ho'oponopono prayer.

Similar to EFT, you can also use Ho'oponopono on an emotion, limiting belief, or challenging situation. You can even use it to forgive and heal others, letting go of any suppressed hatred or hostility. It is also a clearing tool to release blocks from your body's energy system.

9. NATURE IS THE SOLUTION

"Earth and sky, woods and fields, lakes and rivers, the mountain and the sea, are excellent schoolmasters, and teach some of us more than we can ever learn from books."
John Lubbock

Because we no longer spend time in nature, we are alienated from our true nature. Mother Earth is the greatest healer. Many of our challenges come from being disconnected from Mother Earth in the modern world. By spending more time in nature, you can accelerate your healing process.

When I'm in nature, I like to practice earthing, also known as grounding, which involves walking barefoot on the earth's soil or touching it with your bare hands. There are also things like grounding mats, but I believe nothing beats the power of Mother Nature.

Science supports the idea that the earth's electrons create various physiological changes that reduce pain and inflammation, and improve sleep. There is also a shift from the sympathetic to the parasympathetic nervous system and a blood-thinning effect.[3]

The sympathetic nervous system is what activates the fight-or-flight response, which causes anxiety, while the parasympathetic nervous system calms the body. We are electrical, vibrational beings, and by using earthing, we can discharge anxiety, stress, tension, and negative vibes.

Our environment also contains a lot of radiation from technology such as phones and WiFi that we also take on energetically. The earth's electrons clear that from our bodies. That's why you feel so relaxed on holiday because you are in nature, barefoot on the beach and in the sea. You are literally grounding yourself. Mother Gaia is more than willing to heal you, for she knows that when we heal ourselves, we are also healing her at the same time.

With all the tools I'm sharing, there is an abundance of health benefits that are scientifically proven. I'm just not that into science, personally. I like to dive deep into things, experiment and see how I feel. That's what I started doing with anxiety as I saw it as a calling to go within and evolve personally and

---

[3] Chevalier, G., Sinatra, S.T., Oschman, J.L., Sokal, K. and Sokal, P. (2012). Earthing: Health Implications of Reconnecting the Human Body to the Earth's Surface Electrons. *Journal of Environmental and Public Health*, 2012, pp.1–8.

spiritually. Science comes from the mind and does not accurately describe reality.

During my anxiety recovery journey, I went to a Neuro-Linguistic Programming (NLP) practitioner seminar to learn more about life in the hopes of healing myself. One of the tenets of NLP is that 'the map is not the territory.' This basically means that we all form maps of what we think is real, which we then project onto our reality. But our maps are often inaccurate and based on the societal conditioning and programming we have received. That's why we often don't achieve our goals because we have the wrong maps for accomplishing them.

Virtually all maps we carry as of right now collectively are inaccurate. That's why spiritual growth is often about unlearning most of what we have been taught.

My intention with this book is to provide you with a proven map for recovery because the mainstream maps out there are heavily misguided. It's insane that we are told that we cannot recover because the truth is that we can. Science is also a map and comes from the mind, which we know can be inherently limited. Data and science can also be heavily manipulated and misrepresented. Also, the beliefs of the scientist conducting the experiment influence the outcome via the law of attraction.

You can find data to support any conclusion. This is also known as confirmation bias, which is one of our cognitive biases.

What precedes mind and thought is beingness, awareness, consciousness, or God, to use a more religious term. However, there has been much misunderstanding in religion about what the original teachings were pointing to.

By reconnecting with Mother Nature and engaging in some of the spiritual practices and transformational tools included in this book, we can go beyond our minds. We can transcend suffering, anxiety, negative thoughts, programs, beliefs, and conditioning and access higher faculties such as intuition and greater awareness.

Our intuition is connected directly to the quantum field which surrounds us. The quantum field is like an ocean of love that gives life to everything. It is the universal consciousness or awareness that is our true nature.

In the presence of emotional blocks, it can be difficult to tap into our intuition, but by using the tools in this book, you will be able to access it again. We come back to our true selves and form our own decisions and conclusions about what is right for us in our unique life path.

10. SUCCESS IS A MARATHON

"Life is a marathon, not a sprint."
Phillip C. McGraw

Like life, success in any endeavor is a marathon, not a sprint. On your anxiety recovery journey, you will most likely experience setbacks. It's as if you take two steps forward and one step back. You might feel a lot better and then have a few bad days or weeks.

However, over time, you will experience fewer and fewer setbacks and reach a point where anxiety no longer bothers you. Yes, it might feel uncomfortable or inconvenient, but you will also sense that the journey will be complete soon. You know that you are recovering when you increasingly experience positive moments and wins on your journey.

I've provided you with all the tools you need to recover. One thing to bear in mind is that taking action is key. In the application and implementation lies the transformation. And taking action is always going to be imperfect.

When you start accepting anxiety and facing fear, it will be imperfect. You are literally leaving the comfort zone and embodying a new reality. Success is messy.

Even writing this book is an imperfect action because if I wanted it to be perfect or wait for the ideal time, I would never get it done. I'm stepping outside my comfort zone because I've never written a book before. And I'm welcoming all the doubts and fears associated with it, such as "Who am I to write a book?" or "What will people think of me?" or "Am I good enough?" You see, we tend to be our own worst enemy.

I want you to take a moment and really think about what action you want to take in your life, but you've been holding yourself back because of anxiety. Maybe it's leaving the house, starting some cool project, or traveling somewhere. I encourage you to feel the fear and do it anyway. That's the only way to do it.

You can use the law of attraction and the tools I've shared with you, such as visualization and EFT Tapping. You can even tap on the EFT points while you are visualizing your ideal goals and future to remove the blocks associated with them.

You are a powerful, individual expression of infinite potential. Your DNA contains the cosmic inheritance of the universe itself and vibrates as you and through you.

Breathe it, feel it, heal it, and believe it!

What one person can do, another can too. You can overcome anxiety just like I did. There are many stories out there of people who have recovered, and I've also personally helped others recover.

I have shared the map to recovery with you, but it's up to you to take action and use it to guide you to your destination.

11. AWAKENING

"With everything that has happened to you, you can either feel sorry for yourself or treat what has happened as a gift. Everything is either an opportunity to grow or an obstacle to keep you from growing. You get to choose."
Wayne Dyer.

When I started this journey, I never expected it to turn out this way.

Nowadays, I view anxiety as a blessing in disguise because it put me on the path of personal growth and spirituality. I feel truly grateful as my life has taken on a much more meaningful and deeper quality. Are there still challenges? Yes, but my relationship with them has changed.

Anxiety incentivized me to go deep within, explore, and heal. As a result, my life has been transformed. If I hadn't gone through this experience, I probably would have never woken up.

Approximately two and a half years before writing this book, I went through a spiritual awakening. It happened while I was experimenting with a personal growth practice called NoFap, which involves quitting pornography and masturbation. I decided to take on this challenge and did it for 91 days. At the time of writing, I am 28 years old, and I had been using porn frequently since the age of 14. I thought this was normal, as virtually everyone does it.

A friend of mine kept insisting on me trying the NoFap challenge until I gave in and decided to try it. As I started the 90-day NoFap challenge, where I did not watch porn or engage in any sexual stimulation whatsoever, also known as monk mode, I became aware that I was actually addicted as I experienced withdrawal symptoms and cravings. This was a mind-blowing experience.

I went through a period of extreme fatigue as my neurons were rewiring themselves. The effects of porn on the brain are similar to taking heroin. Needless to say, it was a paradigm-shifting experience. I also experienced way more drive, ambition, and motivation to tackle my goals head-on.

The self-help classic "Think And Grow Rich" by Napoleon Hill talks about the transmutation of sexual desire. He explains how many men don't become more successful until they become older as they are hijacked by sexual desire when younger. Sexual energy is creative energy. It can literally create new life.

As I went through the NoFap challenge, I noticed how I no longer started objectifying women. Instead,

I started appreciating them for their femininity and beingness rather than just their external, physical appearance. At the same time, I experienced an expansion in my consciousness and the emergence of a presence that was beyond words. For the first time, I noticed that I am not my thoughts and emotions but rather the awareness that precedes them.

An intense fear accompanied this, which was the ego's fear of dissolution. Our ego is actually an energetic structure within our bodies and minds that takes over. It is the residue of suppressed emotional pain from the past. The only way to heal it is to feel it, so it dissolves in the light of our own awareness.

I think that all the spiritual practice I did combined with NoFap raised my vibration to such a level that it led to a spiritual awakening. In turn, this brought up the ego itself. I just practiced acceptance which I had discovered during anxiety recovery. It truly helped me a lot in that moment of spiritual awakening.

I then went through a few months of emotional purges and releases. I sometimes found myself sleeping for 16 hours, but I knew intuitively that this was the right thing to do. Luckily, I had some social media clients to cover my bills that were easy to handle.

Eventually, the pandemic came along, which we still find ourselves in as I am writing this, and I lost all my clients due to it. My life seemingly broke down, but I sensed that something new was seeking to emerge. Whereas before, I was very much into personal growth, I then became very much more interested in spirituality. I explored all kinds of teachings, books, and philosophies as I found myself in this awakening process that led me to question everything I had ever learned.

While I still experience challenges, negative thoughts and emotions, limiting beliefs, and I definitely still have an ego, I now feel an undercurrent of peace, love, joy, inspiration, and harmony. It's been a wild ride these past few years, but, looking back, it's been a true blessing.

I feel that we have reached a pivotal moment in the evolution of consciousness on this planet. Whether we are aware of it or not, we are all on this spiritual awakening journey. It's the ultimate destiny of each soul, for we are that infinite awareness.

I feel like I've now found my calling, and it is my mission to support others in overcoming anxiety, raising their vibration, and being happy.

12. CASE STUDY

Because I've managed to overcome anxiety, I've decided to use my experience to help others achieve the same result. You might think that I am some special case and that it may not work for you, but I am confident that it can.

Around a year ago, before writing this book, I decided to become a coach, and subsequently, I have also managed to help others overcome anxiety.

Below is an image of Murray Bladen, one of my coaching clients from New Zealand who was struggling with anxiety after a relationship breakup.
We decided to work together, and after just two months, he started feeling recovered, positive, and wonderful. He also now has the tools, understanding, and insights to handle whatever life may throw at him.

I just wanted to share this story to show you that you can do the same.

Remember that you are powerful beyond measure!

13. CONCLUSION

I want to share a quick checklist with you to help you implement what you've learned in this book.

Start your day in the following way:

1. Wake up and get out of bed
2. Open the window and breathe in some fresh air
3. Drink a glass of water with some lemon
4. Do some stretching, yoga, or Qigong
5. Do three rounds of Wim Hof breathing
6. Go for a shower and run the water cold for the last 30 seconds
7. 5-10 Minutes of Meditation
8. Visualize your dreams and ideal life as already being real
9. Practice gratitude and affirmations
10. Read an empowering self-help book, even if it's just a few pages

I am confident that implementing this will change your life over time.

Remember that transformation takes time and effort, so do not expect instant results and give up after a few days. It can take a couple of weeks to feel the difference.

When you feel anxious throughout the day, accept it as best as you can while keeping busy so that you don't obsess about it.

Don't google symptoms. Do the things you are afraid of, even if there is anxiety. Additionally, make sure to rest and take it easy.

If you cannot sleep in the evening, listen to some nature sounds or guided sleeping meditations. You can download these online and play them on your laptop or cellphone.

You could also download my FREE Guided Meditation For Anxiety Relief in case you haven't done so yet. You can download it by visiting: andykloss.com/book-gift

What can also be helpful is to just focus on the breath until you fall asleep. This can anchor you in the present moment and was my personal approach to being able to sleep. It's also essential to accept not being able to sleep because this ironically brings sleep closer.

Acceptance is the most important thing during anxiety recovery.

Make sure you reconnect with Mother Nature.

Thanks for reading my book and I hope that it has been of value to you.

It would mean the world to me if you could share a positive review on Amazon as this helps me spread the message and support more people.

thank you

"*Adversity is the source of our deepest growth and greatest blessings; embrace it, dare to seek it*"
Aron Ralston

BONUS

This book has shown you how I overcame anxiety naturally.

If you resonate with my approach and want me to help you implement it personally, I'd be super excited to see you in my coaching program.

You can sign up on my website under andykloss.com for a FREE Strategy Call where we will look at your unique situation and show you how this system can work for you, too.

Speak to you soon,

Andy

Printed in Great Britain
by Amazon